EXPLORING COUNTRIES
Vietnam

by Walter Simmons

BELLWETHER MEDIA • MINNEAPOLIS, MN

Note to Librarians, Teachers, and Parents:

Blastoff! Readers are carefully developed by literacy experts and combine standards-based content with developmentally appropriate text.

Level 1 provides the most support through repetition of high-frequency words, light text, predictable sentence patterns, and strong visual support.

Level 2 offers early readers a bit more challenge through varied simple sentences, increased text load, and less repetition of high-frequency words.

Level 3 advances early-fluent readers toward fluency through increased text and concept load, less reliance on visuals, longer sentences, and more literary language.

Level 4 builds reading stamina by providing more text per page, increased use of punctuation, greater variation in sentence patterns, and increasingly challenging vocabulary.

Level 5 encourages children to move from "learning to read" to "reading to learn" by providing even more text, varied writing styles, and less familiar topics.

Whichever book is right for your reader, Blastoff! Readers are the perfect books to build confidence and encourage a love of reading that will last a lifetime!

This edition first published in 2011 by Bellwether Media, Inc.

No part of this publication may be reproduced in whole or in part without written permission of the publisher. For information regarding permission, write to Bellwether Media, Inc., Attention: Permissions Department, 5357 Penn Avenue South, Minneapolis, MN 55419.

Library of Congress Cataloging-in-Publication Data
Simmons, Walter (Walter G.)
Vietnam / by Walter Simmons.
   p. cm. — (Exploring countries) (Blastoff! readers)
Includes bibliographical references and index.
Summary: "Developed by literacy experts for students in grades three through seven, this book introduces young readers to the geography and culture of Vietnam"–Provided by publisher.
ISBN 978-1-60014-492-9 (hardcover : alk. paper)
1. Vietnam–Juvenile literature. I. Title.
DS556.3.S537 2010
959.7–dc22   2010017870

Printed in the United States of America, North Mankato, MN.

080110   1162

Contents

Vietnam is a long, narrow country in Southeast Asia. It covers 127,881 square miles (331,210 square kilometers), stretching 1,025 miles (1,650 kilometers) from north to south. The narrowest part of the country is only 31 miles (50 kilometers) across. The capital of Vietnam is Hanoi, a city on the west bank of the Red River.

Vietnam borders three countries. Its northern neighbor is China. To the west are Laos and Cambodia. In the south, a small part of Vietnam reaches the **Gulf** of Thailand. Vietnam also has a long eastern coastline along the South China Sea. The northeastern coast faces the Gulf of Tonkin.

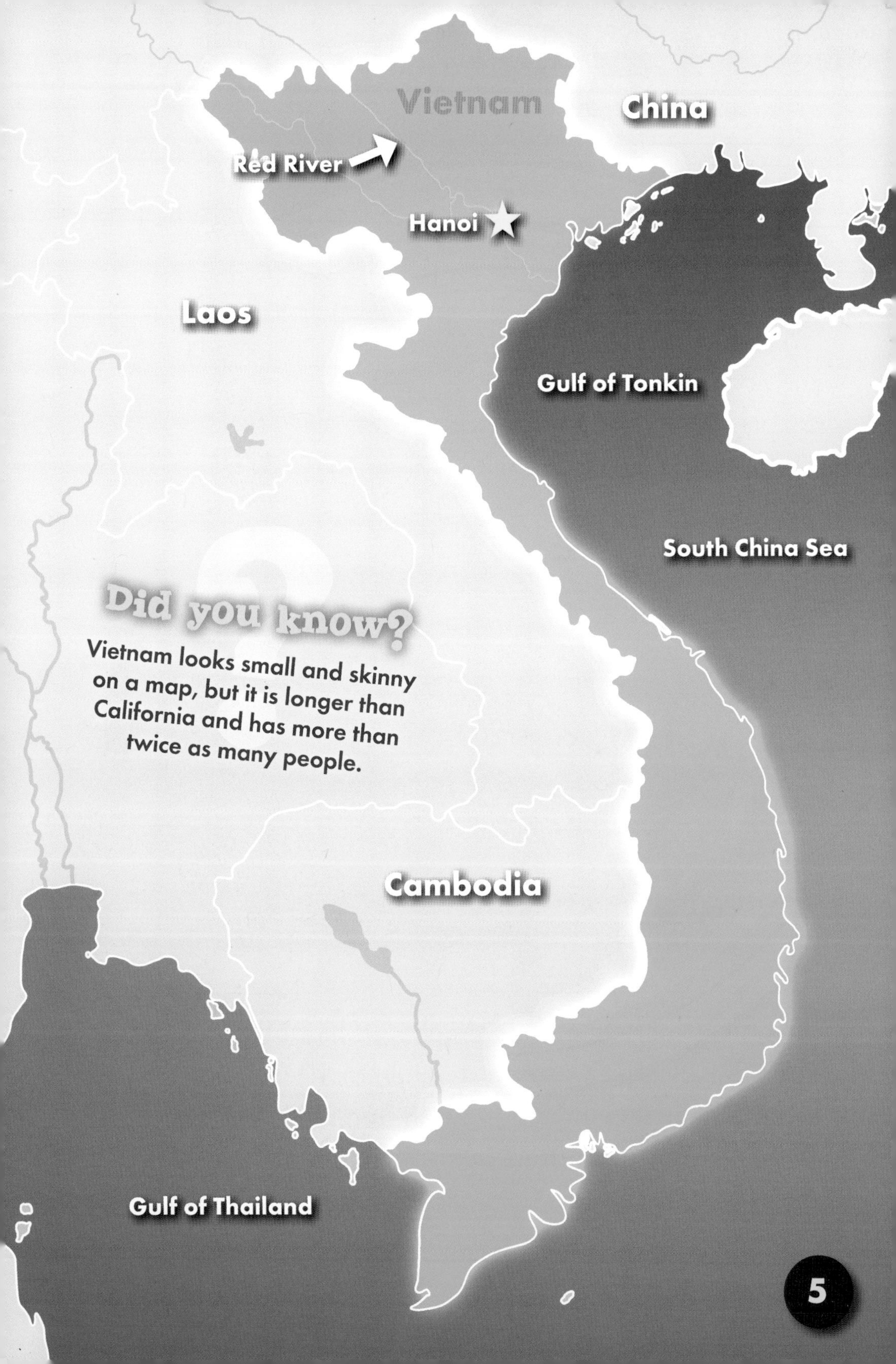

China

Vietnam

Red River

Hanoi ★

Laos

Gulf of Tonkin

South China Sea

Did you know?

Vietnam looks small and skinny on a map, but it is longer than California and has more than twice as many people.

Cambodia

Gulf of Thailand

Vietnam is a mountainous country. Its highest point is Phan Si Pan, which rises to a height of 10,312 feet (3,143 meters) in the Hoang Lien Son mountain range. The Central Highlands lie in the southern half of Vietnam. **Rain forests** cover river valleys and mountains.

Vietnam's mountains slope down to green hills and plains.
Sandy beaches line the coast on the South China Sea.
In the north, the Red River branches into a wide **delta**.
The muddy Mekong River flows through southern Vietnam.
The southern tip of Vietnam is the Ca Mau **Cape**.

Ha Long Bay, or Descending Dragon Bay, opens into the Gulf of Tonkin. More than 3,000 steep pillars and small islands rise out of the bay. According to a legend, a family of dragons created these **limestone** formations. The dragons came to Ha Long Bay to protect the Vietnamese from a Chinese invasion. They spat **jade** and jewels into the sea, shielding the nation with a barrier of stone.

Scientists think Ha Long Bay formed because of **erosion**. They believe rain and waves wore away the limestone over millions of years. Many of the formations have large caves that people enjoy exploring.

! fun fact

There are four fishing villages in Ha Long Bay. Since there is no flat land to build upon, the houses are designed to float on the water.

douc langur

> ! **fun fact**
> The Vietnamese trap poisonous snakes for food, medicine, and snake wine, a drink that is believed to be good for one's health.

Vietnam has many forms of wildlife, including a variety of birds. Wild pheasants, parrots, and partridges nest in the **lowlands**. Herons, cranes, and pelicans live along the seacoasts. Some of these birds **migrate** during the winter. The rain forests of Vietnam are home to tigers, wild boars, Asian elephants, and the Javan rhinoceros. Macaques, lemurs, and douc langurs play in the treetops.

gaur

Asiatic black bear

Asian elephant

Small herds of gaur also roam through the forests. The gaur is the largest species of wild cattle in the world. The Asiatic black bear, or moon bear, and the Malayan sun bear are two kinds of bears that can be found in Vietnam. However, the Asiatic black bear population is falling and the bear is in danger of **extinction**.

The People

Over 89 million people live in Vietnam. The cities, river valleys, and lowlands are very crowded. Mountainous areas have only a few villages and farms. Vietnam is home to more than 50 different groups of people. After the Vietnamese, the largest group is the Tay, who live in the north. Hmong, Chinese, Khmer, and Tai people also live in Vietnam.

Speak Vietnamese!

The Vietnamese language is tonal.
The meaning of a word changes with the
rising, falling, or steady tone of the speaker.

English	Vietnamese	How to say it
hello	chào	chaow
good-bye	tạm biệt	tahm byet
yes	vâng	fahng
no	không	hohng
please	làm ơn	lahm ohn
thank you	cảm ơn bạn	kahm ohn bahn
friend	bạn	bahn

! fun fact

At one time, Vietnam was a colony of France. Some older Vietnamese people still speak French.

The Degar people are **native** to the Central Highlands of Vietnam. They speak their own languages and make up about 30 different tribes. Vietnamese is the country's official language.

Did you know?
Most Vietnamese people still live in the countryside and farm the land. Some live in huts made of bamboo, the fastest-growing woody plant on Earth.

For many Vietnamese people, the day begins with a ride to work or school. In cities, most people use motorbikes or buses to get around. In the countryside, farmers rise early in the morning to go to work in their fields. The afternoon is the hottest part of the day. Many people go home for the midday meal. They eat and cool off before returning to work.

Where People Live in Vietnam

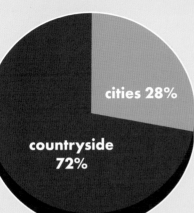

cities 28%

countryside 72%

In the evening, cities are crowded with people strolling and shopping. They can relax in cafés with a coffee or a glass of juice. Many cafés stay open late. In the countryside, many people go to bed soon after the sun sets.

All children in Vietnam must attend elementary school. They start school at the age of 6 and continue for five years. They study reading, writing, math, and history. After elementary school, students may choose to move on to four years of middle school. However, many Vietnamese families cannot afford further schooling for their children. If students continue, they must pass tests to enter a high school or vocational school. High school students take courses in science, math, history, **civics**, and geography. If high school graduates want to go to university, they must take a series of tests. Only about one out of four students goes on to attend university.

fun fact

In Vietnam, students are in charge of cleaning their classrooms. Groups of students take turns showing up early to school to clean.

Where People Work in Vietnam

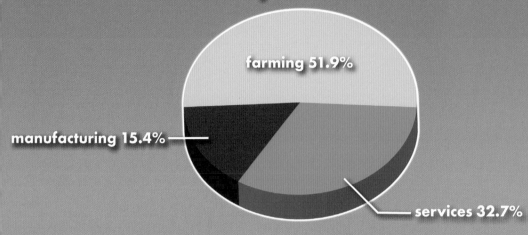

farming 51.9%

manufacturing 15.4%

services 32.7%

Did you know?

Vietnam is one of the world's biggest producers of cashews. It sells more than 150,000 tons of this sweet nut to other countries every year.

Vietnam has a growing economy. Factory workers in the cities make clothing, shoes, cement, and fertilizers. Many foreign companies **invest** in new factories in Vietnam that make computers and electronic equipment.

Most Vietnamese people earn a living from the land. Farmers grow rice, cotton, tea, sugarcane, and peanuts. Some raise cattle, water buffalo, pigs, and chickens. Fish farms supply shrimp and fish to markets and restaurants. Rubber **plantations** send materials to factories where rubber goods like tires are made. Vietnam also has a growing coffee industry. The country sells most of its coffee to the United States.

karate

In Vietnam, people like to play competitive games. These include soccer, badminton, ping-pong, and volleyball. Many kids study **martial arts**. They attend classes to learn and practice *judo*, *karate*, and other fighting styles. Along the coasts, many Vietnamese people swim and surf.

The Vietnamese often visit friends and family in the evenings. People gather to talk, play cards, sing karaoke, or watch television. City cafés are good places to meet with friends, watch people on the street, or play a game of chess, which is a favorite of many Vietnamese people.

fun fact

Fish sauce is used to flavor many Vietnamese dishes. It is made from the juice of mashed-up fish!

The Vietnamese cook noodles, rice, fresh vegetables, and many kinds of seafood and meat. To flavor their dishes, they use **herbs** and chilies. *Pho* is a favorite soup made with meat or fish, noodles, basil, bean sprouts, and lime. Another common meal is *bánh mì*. This is a sandwich made with sliced meat, cucumbers, radishes, carrots, and an herb called cilantro.

People in Vietnam usually eat three meals a day. They start with a light breakfast of soup, rice, or bread. At midday, they eat a small meal. In the evening, many families gather for dinner around a hot cooking pot, or *lau*. Meat, shrimp, and vegetables are ready to be boiled and dipped in tasty sauces.

bánh mì

pho

Did you know?

When preparing a dish, Vietnamese cooks try to include spicy, sour, bitter, salty, and sweet flavors. They also try to use the five traditional colors, which are white, green, yellow, red, and black. Both of these traditions are based on the five elements, which are wood, fire, earth, metal, and water.

The most important holiday in Vietnam is *Tet Nguyen Dan*, or *Tet* for short. This is the Vietnamese New Year, celebrated with feasts and gifts. The holiday lasts for several days. The Vietnamese also observe many other national holidays. On May 19, they celebrate the birthday of Ho Chi Minh, a famous Vietnamese leader. Independence Day is celebrated on September 2. This marks the day in 1945 when Ho Chi Minh declared Vietnam's independence from France.

In 2007, Vietnam created a new holiday celebrating the Hung kings. These kings ruled ancient Vietnam. They established a **dynasty** that lasted for more than 2,000 years. The Hung Kings' Temple Festival takes place in April.

Did you know?

Vietnamese people do not celebrate their birthdays on the days they were born. Instead, they all celebrate their birthdays on the same day–*Tet*!

Tet Nguyen Dan

In 1975, Vietnam adopted a form of government called **communism**. By the 1980s, Vietnam was a very poor country. Under communism, the Vietnamese government took control of every business. Foreign companies could not sell their goods to or invest in Vietnam. Many factories closed, and it was hard for people to buy what they needed.

In 1986, the government began a new system called *Doi
Moi*, which means "change." Foreign companies could build
new factories and sell products in Vietnam. Since then, it
has been easier for Vietnamese people to find jobs and buy
the goods they need. *Doi Moi* has played a huge role in
improving Vietnam's economy and reconnecting the country
with the rest of the world.

Fast Facts About Vietnam

Vietnam's Flag

The flag of Vietnam is red with a five-pointed yellow star in the center. The red color represents blood, revolution, and the Communist party, and the yellow color represents Vietnam. The five points of the star stand for the country's peasants, workers, intellectuals, traders, and soldiers. In 1975, this flag was adopted as the new national flag.

Official Name: Socialist Republic of Vietnam

Area: 127,881 square miles (331,210 square kilometers); Vietnam is the 65th largest country in the world.

Capital City:	Hanoi
Important Cities:	Ho Chi Minh City, Haiphong, Hue, Da Nang, Can Tho
Population:	89,571,130 (July 2010)
Official Language:	Vietnamese
National Holiday:	Independence Day (September 2)
Religions:	None (80.8%), Buddhist (9.3%), Other (9.9%)
Major Industries:	farming, fishing, manufacturing, mining, services
Natural Resources:	bauxite, coal, crude oil, gold, iron ore, salt, tin, zinc
Manufactured Products:	appliances, cement, glass, electronics, fertilizers, steel, rubber products
Farm Products:	coffee, tea, rubber, rice, soybeans, sugarcane, peanuts, chickens, cattle, pigs
Unit of Money:	dong

Glossary

cape—part of a coastline that sticks out into the sea

civics—studies related to being a good citizen of a country or community

communism—a form of government where the government controls all resources and business in a country

delta—the area around the mouth of a river

dynasty—a group of rulers from one family line

erosion—the slow wearing away of soil or rock by water or wind

extinction—when every member of a species has died off

gulf—part of an ocean or sea that extends into land

herbs—plants used in cooking; people use herbs to add flavor to food.

invest—to give money to a person or business now in order to make more money later

jade—a hard, green stone often used to make sculptures and jewelry

limestone—rock that forms over millions of years from the remains of shells and corals; limestone is often used in construction.

lowlands—areas of land that are lower than the surrounding land

martial arts—styles and techniques of fighting and self-defense

migrate—to move from one place to another, often with the seasons

native—originally from a place

plantations—large farms that grow coffee, cotton, rubber, or other crops; plantations are mainly found in warm climates.

rain forests—thick forests that receive a lot of rain

To Learn More

AT THE LIBRARY

Garland, Sherry. *Children of the Dragon: Selected Tales from Vietnam*. San Diego, Calif.: Harcourt, 2001.

Green, Jen. *Vietnam*. Washington, D.C.: National Geographic, 2008.

Willis, Terri. *Vietnam*. New York, N.Y.: Children's Press, 2002.

ON THE WEB

Learning more about Vietnam is as easy as 1, 2, 3.

1. Go to www.factsurfer.com.

2. Enter "Vietnam" into the search box.

3. Click the "Surf" button and you will see a list of related Web sites.

With factsurfer.com, finding more information is just a click away.

Index

The images in this book are reproduced through the courtesy of: Scott Truesdale, front cover, pp. 8 (small), 11 (top), 14, 18; Maisei Raman, front cover (flag), p. 28; Jon Eppard, pp. 4-5; Robert Francis/ Photolibrary, pp. 6-7; Jean Rey/Photolibrary, pp. 8-9; Anup Shah/Photolibrary, pp. 10-11; Better Stock, p. 11 (middle); imagebroker/Alamy, p. 11 (bottom); Stu Smucker/Photolibrary, p. 12; Walter Bibikow/ Photolibrary, p. 15; Jorgen Schytte/Photolibrary, pp. 16-17, 22; Gerhard Zwerger-Schoner/Photolibrary, p. 19 (top); Joachim E Röttgers/Photolibrary, p. 19 (bottom); AFP/Getty Images, pp. 20, 26 (small); Mauro Ladu/Alamy, p. 21; 123stocks, p. 23 (top); Brian Weed, p. 23 (bottom); JTB Photo/Photolibrary, pp. 24-25; Thein Do/Photolibrary, pp. 26-27; Anibal Trejo, p. 29 (bill); Wikipedia, p. 29 (coin).